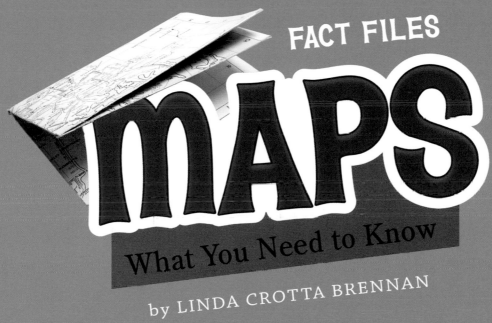

First Facts®

FACT FILES

MAPS

What You Need to Know

by LINDA CROTTA BRENNAN

CAPSTONE PRESS
a capstone imprint

First Facts are published by Capstone Press,
1710 Roe Crest Drive, North Mankato, Minnesota 56003
www.mycapstone.com

Library of Congress Cataloging-in-Publication Data
Library of Congress Cataloging-in-Publication data is available on the Library of Congress website.
ISBN 978-1-5157-8109-7 (library binding)
ISBN 978-1-5157-8122-6 (paperback)
ISBN 978-1-5157-8130-1 (eBook PDF)

Editorial Credits
Mandy Robbins, editor; Jenny Bergstrom, designer; Kelly Garvin, media researcher; Laura Manthe, production specialist

Photo Credits
Shutterstock: Artlisticco, 13, Betacam-SP, 9 (bottom right), Cvijun, 7, dikobraziy, 21, Dja65, 4, dvoevnore, 8, Eka Panova, 6, ergonomal, cover (top right), 19, freesoulproduction, cover (top left), Globe Turner, 9 (bottom left), HomeStudio, cover (br), 1, lcatnews, 5, mstudioVector, 15, Oleksandr Berezko, 17, oxameel, 9 (tl), pablofdezr, 9 (tr), pavalena, 11, Peter Hermes Furian, 15, prokopphoto, 24, Scanrail1, 3, Triff, cover (bl), Zmiter, backcover, 12

Printed in China.
010295F17

Table of Contents

Introduction to Maps

Where are you right now? Where do you want to go next? A map can help you get there.

A map is a drawing of what an area looks like from above. Maps use lines, colors, and pictures to tell you about a place.

FACT

A stone tablet in northern Spain may be the world's oldest map. Scientists think it is about 14,000 years old.

4

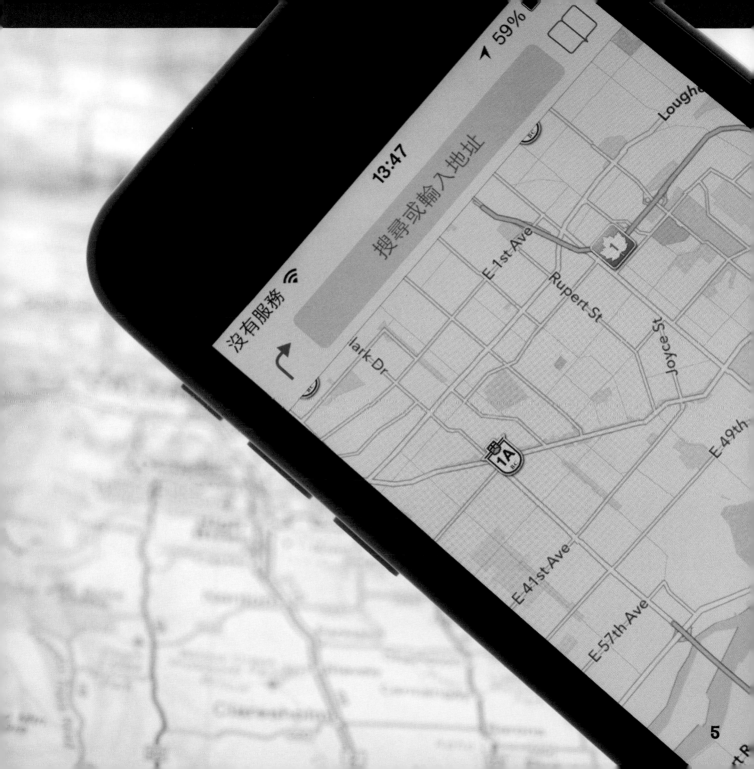

Types of Maps

You couldn't use a map of Earth to find your way around school. To get where you need to go, you must have the right map.

Some maps show the whole world or an entire country. But what if you want to find the local hospital? For that you need a map of your city or town.

WORLD MAP

A MAP'S

TITLE

TELLS YOU WHAT
IT IS ABOUT.

**THIS MAP SHOWS ALL THE
COUNTRIES OF THE WORLD.**

CAN YOU FIND THE COUNTRY
YOU LIVE IN?

There are many types of maps. Political maps show countries. Road maps show roads and cities. Historical maps show what places looked like long ago. There are also maps of the sea and the stars.

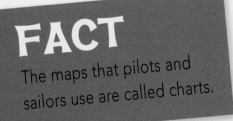

FACT
The maps that pilots and sailors use are called charts.

SEA CHART

STAR CHART

POLITICAL MAP

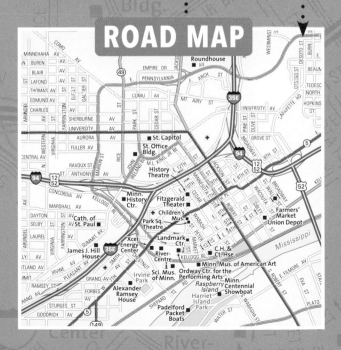

ROAD MAP

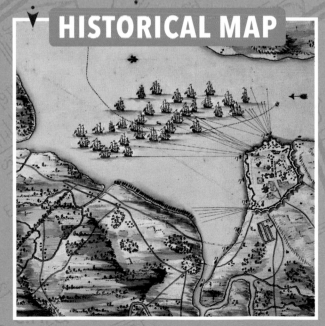

HISTORICAL MAP

Parts of a Map

Maps use colors and symbols to give information. A map's **key** tells you what its colors and symbols mean. On most maps, blue means water.

Some maps show **elevation**. Brown means highlands. Yellow and orange stand for middle lands. Green means low lands.

key—a list or chart that explains the colors and symbols on a map
elevation—the height of the land above sea level

MAP OF GERMANY

WHICH CITY IS THE

CAPITAL

OF GERMANY?

NAME A

RIVER

IN GERMANY.

KEY

⌇ RIVER
● CITY
★ CAPITAL CITY

Most maps have **compass roses**.
A compass rose is a circle with arrows that
split it into four equal parts. The arrows
point in the directions north, east, south,
and west.

compass rose—a label that
shows the directions north,
east, south, and west on a map
compass—an instrument used
for finding directions

KEY

Entrance	Horses	Tigers
Fountain	Camels	Cheetahs
Bathrooms	Birds	Flamingos
Food	Turtles	Snakes
Monkeys	Hippos	
Rhinos	Lions	

SEARCH

You are at the zoo by the lions. You want to see the monkeys. Should you go north, east, south, or west?

Maps are smaller than the places they show. The map's *scale* tells you how much smaller the map is than real life.

Some maps have **grids** to help you find a place. Grids are evenly spaced lines that run up-and-down and side-to-side.

scale—a label on the map that compares the distances on a map and the actual distances on Earth
grid—a pattern of evenly spaced, or parallel, lines that cross

On this map each inch in the grid equals 500 miles.

MEASURE

the inches between Alice Springs and Mackay.

HOW MANY

miles are there between the two towns? Mackay is in section 6C. In what

SECTION

of the grid is Alice Springs?

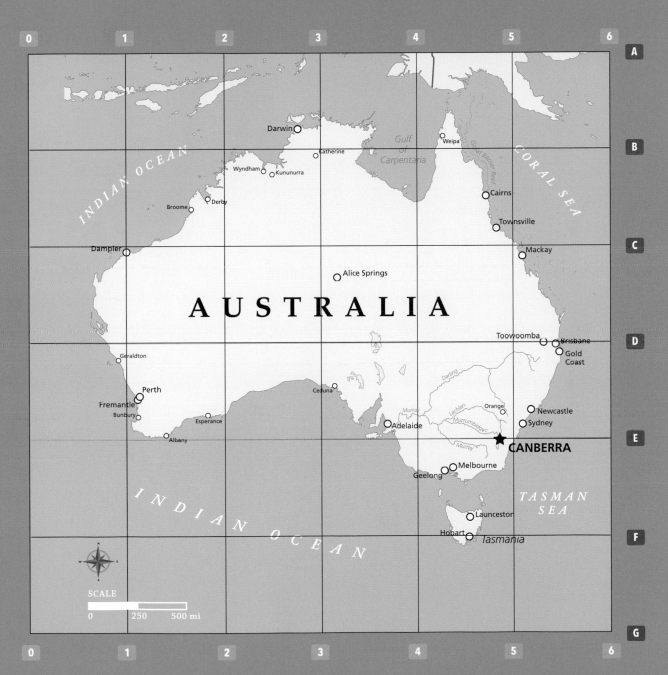

Maps of the World

Most maps are flat. It makes them easy to fold up and carry. But the world is shaped like a ball. To make a world map flat, countries are shown stretched and pulled out of shape. A *globe* is a map that shows Earth's round shape. It gives a more true picture of Earth.

FACT
There are seven **continents** on Earth: Africa, Antarctica, Asia, Australia, Europe, North America, and South America.

globe—a round model of the world
continent—one of the seven large landmasses of Earth

16

A globe has special lines. Those that run up-and-down are lines of **longitude**. Those that run sideways are lines of **latitude**. The line around the center of the globe is called the **equator**. The point at the top of the globe is the North Pole. The point at the bottom is the South Pole.

longitude—the position of a place, measured in degrees east or west of an imaginary line that runs through Greenwich, England
latitude—the position of a place, measured in degrees north or south of the equator
equator—an imaginary line around the middle of Earth; it divides the northern and southern hemispheres

NORTH POLE

LATITUDE LINES

EQUATOR

LONGITUDE LINES

SOUTH POLE

Try to Find It

Maps can help you find your way on land, at sea, or even in space. So grab a map and explore!

Earth has four oceans. They are the Arctic, Atlantic, Indian, and Pacific oceans. Can you find the Atlantic Ocean on this world map?

Australia is east of the Indian Ocean. Can you find both on this map?

On what continent is Mount Everest?

ANSWER: Mount Everest is in Asia.

WORLD MAP

ARCTIC OCEAN

NORTH AMERICA

Rocky Mountains

Mississippi River

ATLANTIC OCEAN

PACIFIC OCEAN

Amazon River

SOUTH AMERICA

Andes Mountains

EUROPE

AFRICA

Ural Mountains

ASIA

Mount Everest

INDIAN OCEAN

AUSTRALIA

ANTARCTICA

KEY

- WATER
- MOUNTAINS
- RIVER
- MOUNT

Glossary

compass (KUHM-puhs)—an instrument used for finding directions

compass rose (KUHM-puhs ROHZ)—a label that shows direction on a map

continent (KON-tuh-nuhnt)—one of the seven large landmasses of Earth

elevation (e-luh-VAY-shuhn)—the height of the land above sea level

equator (i-KWAY-tuhr)—an imaginary line around the middle of Earth

globe (GLOHB)—a round model of the world

grid (GRID)—a pattern of evenly spaced, or parallel, lines that cross

key (KEE)—a list or chart that explains colors or symbols on a map

latitude (LAT-uh-tood)—the distance measured north or south of the equator

longitude (LON-juh-tood)—the distance measured east or west of a line that runs through Greenwich, England; lines of longitude are drawn from the North Pole to the South Pole

scale (SKALE)—a label on the map that compares the distances on a map and the actual distances on Earth

Read More

Matzke, Ann. *Reading Maps.* Little World Social Studies. Vero Beach, Fla.: Rourke Educational Media, 2013.

Rajczak, Kristen. *Types of Maps.* Map Basics. New York: Gareth Stevens Publishing, 2015.

Waldron, Melanie. *Types of Maps.* Let's Get Mapping! Chicago: Raintree, 2013.

Internet Sites

Use FactHound find Internet sites related to this book.

Visit *www.facthound.com*

Just type in 9781515781097

Check out projects, games and lots more at
www.capstonekids.com

Critical Thinking Questions

1. What kind of map shows states and countries?

2. What parts of a map can be found on the map on page 11?

3. On a world map, find the country where you live. Would it take longer for you to travel to Spain or to Mexico? How do you know?

Index